nd all the world explore. I know that a

ure may some light unfold

And soar from

rove, my calling to pursue, Or mount up f

an do. My genius from a boy, Has fluttere

o depart. She like a restless bird, Would spread her wing,

s be loudly heard, And dart from world to world

Poet

The Remarkable Story of George Moses Horton

To my sweet mom, Sharon Tate,
and to my grandchildren, Charles, Kordelle,
Aniyah, and Zoee, who all love words.
—D. T.

Ω

Published by
PEACHTREE PUBLISHERS
1700 Chattahoochee Avenue
Atlanta, Georgia 30318-2112
www.peachtree-online.com

Book design by Don Tate
Composition by Loraine M. Joyner
Illustrations are mixed media: gouache, archival ink, and pencil on
acid-free, 100% cotton watercolor paper, and digital. Text is typeset in
International Typeface Corporation's Caxton Book by Leslie Usherwood
for Letraset. Title, subtitle, byline, Horton's poems, and endpapers
are hand-lettered by Don Tate.

Printed in October 2016 by Tien Wah Press in Malaysia
10 9 8 7 6 5 4 3

Library of Congress Cataloging-in-Publication Data

Tate, Don.
Poet : the remarkable story of George Moses Horton / Don Tate.
pages cm
ISBN 978-1-56145-825-7
Includes bibliographical references.
1. Horton, George Moses, 1798?-approximately 1880—Juvenile
literature. 2. Poets, American—19th century—Biography—Juvenile
literature. 3. African American poets—Biography—Juvenile literature. 4.
Slaves—North Carolina—Biography—Juvenile literature. 5. Freedmen—
United States—Biography—Juvenile literature. I. Title.
PS1999.H473Z88 2015
811'.4—dc23
[B]
                    2015002407

Poet

The Remarkable Story of George Moses Horton

Don Tate

PEACHTREE
ATLANTA

GEORGE LOVED WORDS. He wanted to learn how to read, but George was enslaved. He and his family lived on a farm in Chatham County, North Carolina, where they were forced to work long hours. There wasn't time for much else. Besides, George knew his master would not approve of his slaves reading.

But that didn't stop George from admiring the language that was all around him: Inspirational words read from the Bible. Hopeful words delivered in a sermon. Lively words sung in songs.

George was determined to learn how to read. When white children studied their books, he lingered nearby. He listened as they repeated the letters of the alphabet.

Soon, George could recite the alphabet himself.

His mother would have liked to help him, but she couldn't. Instead, she gave George one of her most valuable possessions: a Wesley hymnal, a book of songs.

It was George's very first book! He scanned the pages, trying to make out the letters. It was no use, though; he could not read the words.

Then George found an old spelling book. It was tattered and some pages were missing, but it was enough to get him started.

George thumbed through its pages. He recognized some of the letters.

At night, when he should have been resting after a long day of work, George studied by firelight. His eyes burned from the smoke.

Soon he could make out a few words.

Before long he could understand entire sentences.

Over time, George taught himself to read.

From that point forward, George not only loved words,
he could read and understand them too. George read verses
from the New Testament. He read books, newspaper articles,
advertisements—whatever he could find.

Most of all, George read poems. He loved beautiful poetry.

Rise up, my soul and let us go
up to the gospel feast . . .

From early morning until late at night, George tended cattle on his master's farm. While he worked, George composed his own poetry, mingling his words with the tunes of familiar songs. He hadn't learned how to write his poems down yet, so he committed them to memory. Words and rhythms were stored up inside his head.

His verses swayed with emotion, like the music of Sunday services. They kept him strong as he grew to be a young man.

When George was seventeen, his master decided to split up his estate. He divided his possessions—land, cattle, wagons, tools—among his family. Slaves were considered to be property too, so George's family was separated.

George was given to his master's son. He feared he would never see his mother, brothers, and sisters again.

George toiled in the fields on his new master's property. It was disagreeable work, but he found a little relief on Sundays. On that day, George walked eight miles to the village of Chapel Hill, to the campus of the University of North Carolina. There, he sold fruit and vegetables grown on his master's farm.

He didn't mind the long walk, though. George welcomed the opportunity to get away.

At first, the college students teased George. To distract himself from their insults, George recited his poetry. Words, sweet as the fruit piled high in his cart, sprung from his lips.

Every eye grew wide and every mouth fell open at the sound of George's voice, uttering beautiful verses. The students were awestruck when they found out that he had composed them himself.

News of the slave poet raced through campus like a brisk-flowing river. Students swarmed in close to hear George perform his verses.

Some of them decided to help George. They gave him their books: English grammar and dictionaries. History and oratory. Classic literature and poetry.

George soaked up these new subjects like a sponge.

One day, a student requested a poem for his sweetheart.
George created a verse for the woman. He dictated the poem
to the student, who wrote it out neatly.

The young lady swooned when she read it.

After that, other students wanted George's poems. And
they were willing to pay for them too.

George composed more than a dozen love poems a week, selling them for 25 cents each. Some paid him with fine suits and shoes instead of money. In time, George dressed as sharply as the students themselves.

With money, nice clothes, and newfound status, George felt freer than he ever had in all of his life.

But he was not free. He remained the property of his master. George continued to work on the farm during the week and visit Chapel Hill on the weekends.

The story of the slave poet reached the wife of a professor. Caroline Lee Hentz was a professional writer and published poet. George's poems affected her deeply. Some made her smile, while others made her cry.

She sought out George and taught him how to write his poems on paper with a pen. After so many years of memorizing verses, George could now write them down.

Caroline arranged for George's poems to be printed in the *Gazette*, the newspaper of her hometown, Lancaster, Massachusetts. Now George was a published poet.

His poems protested his enslavement. No other American slave had done that before.

Soon George's work appeared in other newspapers, including *Freedom's Journal*, the first African-American-owned newspaper in the country.

George's heart could barely contain his growing pride.

With money from his writing and odd jobs, George was able to pay

his master for his time, so that he could live in Chapel Hill and work

as a poet. It was an illegal arrangement, but his master didn't care.

George was now a full-time writer, but he was still not a free man.

In time, George published THE HOPE OF LIBERTY, his first book. He wanted to use his earnings to purchase his freedom.

When editors at *Freedom's Journal* learned of his plan, they tried to raise money to help him. Influential people joined the cause—newspapermen, a college president, a governor. They offered a great deal of money, but George's master refused to sell his valuable slave.

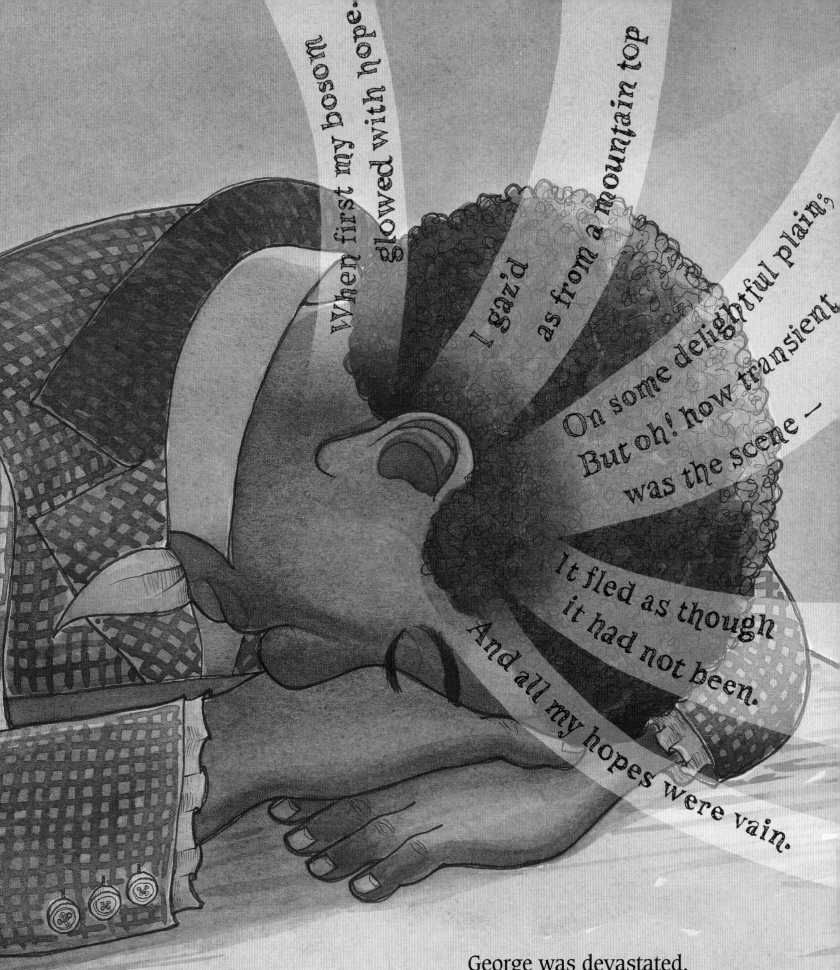

When first my bosom glowed with hope,

I gaz'd as from a mountain top

On some delightful plain;

But oh! how transient was the scene —

It fled as though it had not been.

And all my hopes were vain.

George was devastated.

Meanwhile, abolitionists in the North worked to end slavery. They published books. They printed posters and pamphlets. They blanketed the South with their calls for enslaved people to rise up against their masters. Slaves who could read told others their message.

As a result, more slaves did fight back, and some even killed their masters. Fear ruled the South.

New laws were passed in North Carolina. People who printed and distributed anti-slavery materials were penalized. Worse yet, it became illegal to teach a slave how to read or write.

Now it was too dangerous for George to write poems that protested slavery.

But he didn't stop writing altogether. He published his second book, THE POETICAL WORKS OF GEORGE M. HORTON, which contained poems about life, love, death, and friendship.

In 1861, war broke out between the North and South, mainly over the issue of slavery. Most of the students went off to fight, to defend the South.

With few people left on campus to purchase his poems, George had no way to earn money to pay for his time away from his master. He had to return to the farm.

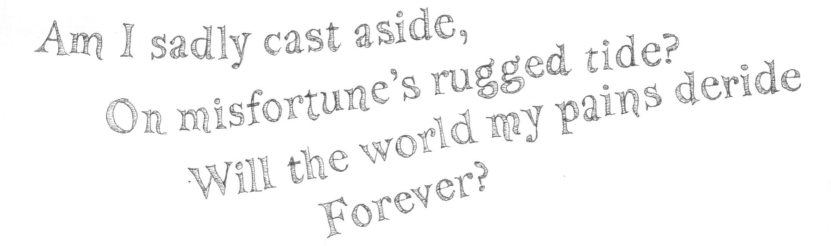

Am I sadly cast aside,
On misfortune's rugged tide?
Will the world my pains deride
Forever?

The Civil War raged on for four long years. In 1863, President Abraham Lincoln set the nation on a new course by signing the Emancipation Proclamation. That soon led to the end of slavery.

At the age of sixty-six, George was finally free!

Now that he was a free man, George no longer had to remain on the farm. Later that spring, he packed his pens and paper and left.

George went west with the Union army, camping along the way. He wrote poems about his travels, about his family and friends back home, and about all the things he had experienced in his long life.

I'll love thee as long as I live,
Whate'er thy condition may be;

All else but my life
That thou wast as p

George's love of words had taken him on a great journey.
Words made him strong. Words allowed him to dream. Words
loosened the chains of bondage long before his last day as a slave.

I found the following books and websites very helpful while I was researching and writing this book. —D. T.

Horton, George Moses. NAKED GENIUS. Chapel Hill, NC: The Chapel Hill Historical Society, 1982.

Horton, George Moses. THE POETICAL WORKS OF GEORGE M. HORTON, THE COLORED BARD OF NORTH-CAROLINA, TO WHICH IS PREFIXED THE LIFE OF THE AUTHOR, WRITTEN BY HIMSELF, GEORGE HORTON. Hillsborough, NC: D. Heartt, 1845.
    This book is available as a free download at *Documenting the South*, a website maintained by the University of North Carolina at Chapel Hill, at *www.docsouth.unc.edu/fpn/hortonpoem/ menu.html*

Sherman, Joan R, eds. THE BLACK BARD OF NORTH CAROLINA: GEORGE MOSES HORTON AND HIS POETRY. Chapel Hill, NC: The University of North Carolina Press, 1997.

Walser, Richard. THE BLACK POET: BEING THE REMARKABLE STORY (PARTLY TOLD MY [sic] HIMSELF) OF GEORGE MOSES HORTON, A NORTH CAROLINA SLAVE. New York: Philosophical Library Inc., 1966.

Walser, Richard and Julia Montgomery Street. NORTH CAROLINA PARADE: STORIES OF HISTORY AND PEOPLE. Chapel Hill, NC: The University of North Carolina Press, 1966.

Williams, Heather Andrea. SELF-TAUGHT: AFRICAN AMERICAN EDUCATION IN SLAVERY AND FREEDOM. Chapel Hill, NC: The University of North Carolina Press, 2005.

The North Carolina Story: A Virtual Museum of University History, The University of North Carolina at Chapel Hill, *www.museum.unc.edu*

Quotations from several of George Moses Horton's poems appear on the endpapers and are incorporated into the artwork throughout this book. Horton's work is now in the public domain and the full text of many of his poems can be found online.

Front endpaper–from "George Moses Horton, Myself," published in NAKED GENIUS in 1865 *www.poetryfoundation.org/poem/185987*

Page 10–from THE POETICAL WORKS OF GEORGE M. HORTON, THE COLORED BARD OF NORTH-CAROLINA, TO WHICH IS PREFIXED THE LIFE OF THE AUTHOR, WRITTEN BY HIMSELF, GEORGE HORTON, published in 1845 *www.docsouth.unc. edu/fpn/hortonpoem/menu.html*

Page 17–from "For The Fair Miss M. M. McL[ean] An acrostic," published somewhere around 1853–1855

Page 25–from "Slavery," published in *Freedom's Journal* in 1828 and *Liberator* in 1834

Page 28–from "The Slave's Complaint," published in THE HOPE OF LIBERTY in 1829 *www.poets.org/poetsorg/poem/slaves-complaint*

Page 32–from "To Catherine" found in THE POETICAL WORKS OF GEORGE M. HORTON, THE COLORED BARD OF NORTH-CAROLINA, TO WHICH IS PREFIXED THE LIFE OF THE AUTHOR, WRITTEN BY HIMSELF, GEORGE HORTON, published in 1845

Back endpapers–from "The Obstruction of Genius," With letter to Horace Greeley, in 1852 *www.ibiblio.org/uncpress/horton/genius.html*

The quotation on pages 4–5 is from Psalm 98:4 in the King James version of the Bible.

AUTHOR'S NOTE

WHEN I FIRST BEGAN illustrating children's books, I decided that I would not work on stories about slavery. I had many reasons, one being that I wanted to focus on contemporary stories relevant to young readers today. In all honesty, though, what I wasn't admitting to myself was that I was ashamed of the topic.

I grew up in a small town in the Midwest in the 1970s and 80s. At school, I was usually the only brown face in a sea of white. It seemed to me that whenever the topic of black history came up, it was always in relation to slavery, about how black people were once the property of white people—no more human than a horse or a wheelbarrow. Sometimes white kids snickered and made jokes about the topic. Sometimes, black kids did too.

As my career progressed, more manuscripts on the topic of slavery were offered to me. At first I hesitated. But as I read the stories and studied the history of my people, I had a change of heart. I decided that there was nothing to be ashamed of, and much to feel proud about.

I fell in love with stories that demonstrated the resilience of African-American people. And although the publishing industry could do a better job of balancing the topic of slavery with other African-American stories, tales of enslaved people deserve to be told.

I was especially intrigued when an author friend suggested I write about George Moses Horton. For research, I relied heavily on Horton's autobiography, THE LIFE OF THE AUTHOR, WRITTEN BY HIMSELF. It's a short, inspiring narrative, outlining the major events of his life. But it raised many questions that nagged at me.

George Moses Horton taught himself to read, sold poetry to college students, and published several books—all at a time when African-American literacy was discouraged, devalued, even outlawed in this country. How was he able to accomplish so much?

To better understand what Horton achieved, I needed to study the unique characteristics of slavery in North Carolina. I learned that things were somewhat different there than they were elsewhere in the South. North Carolina was home to one of the largest free black populations in all of the colonies. Many North Carolinians supported antislavery organizations and the emancipation of slaves. Plantations were smaller, requiring fewer laborers, and often less affluent farmers worked their land alongside their slaves. In fact, as peculiar as this may sound, slaves were sometimes considered family members. No doubt, Horton benefited from this more open-minded atmosphere.

Life for an enslaved person was still not easy in North Carolina. Slaves performed daylong, back-breaking work for no pay. Their diet, provided by their owners, was typically poor, and their clothing inadequate. Families could be torn apart and sold away at any time, never to see each other again—as happened to George. In the face of these adversities, Horton's achievements were monumental.

In 1831, about fifty-five whites were killed in a slave rebellion in nearby Virginia, and attitudes changed in North Carolina. Literate slaves, who could read about abolitionists' activities and inform others, were now a threat. North Carolina passed laws that forbade anyone—white or black—from teaching an enslaved person to read or write. Whites could be fined for breaking the law; a person of color, slave or free, could be whipped—up to thirty-nine lashes!

Needless to say, it was a dangerous time for Horton, whose poems often protested slavery. He continued to write and even published a second book, THE POETICAL WORKS OF GEORGE MOSES HORTON, but he avoided the topic of slavery or his hope for freedom.

Following the end of the Civil War, Horton gained his freedom. In 1865, he published NAKED GENIUS, a third book of poems. In his final years, he moved to Philadelphia, where he wrote short narratives based upon Bible stories, selling them to magazines and Sunday school periodicals. He died in approximately 1883, though the exact date is not known. Nor do we know what he looked like; though you can find photographs on the internet that claim to depict Horton, there are no known images of the poet.

In creating this book, it was my goal to present the topic of slavery as more than just an uncomfortable word. I wanted readers to know who George Moses Horton was, and to demonstrate his relevance in their lives today.

In Horton's day, African-American literacy was unusual—even outlawed. Today, of course, rates are much higher. Still, statistics show that far too many African-American students graduate from high school functionally illiterate—meaning that they cannot read or write. In many ways, literacy is as much of an issue today as it was in Horton's day.

I hope that young readers will see themselves in the story of George Moses Horton—a person with talents and hopes and dreams, and a desire to be free. Just like them.

ACKNOWLEDGMENTS

FOR THEIR ASSISTANCE during the process

of researching this book, I'd like to thank

Earl L. Ijames, Curator, North Carolina Museum of History;

Matt Karkutt, University Libraries, University of North Carolina at Chapel Hill;

Wilson Library, University of North Carolina at Chapel Hill;

the Chapel Hill Historical Society;

and Gregory Tyler, former Curator, Historic Hope Plantation, Windsor, NC.

Thank you to my wonderful editor, Kathy Landwehr, whose sharp eye, quick wit,

and gentle guidance made this bookmaking process nothing short of awesome.

Thank you, Chris Barton, for inspiring me to write this story,

and to my wonderful critique buddies Donna Janell Bowman and Carmen Oliver.

Thank you also to my illustration critique buddies, The Armadillustrators:

Jeff Crosby, Christopher S. Jennings, Thomas Jung, Erik Kuntz, Nick Alter, and Scott Dubois.

urveyed by envy's eye,

By white and colored all

To fee'

oft draws out a secret sigh,

Whi

Genius seemed leading to a to

To urge the nig

Has philan